POWER OF ATTORNEY KIT

M. Stephen Georgas, LLB

Self-Counsel Press
(a division of)
International Self-Counsel Press Ltd.
Canada   USA

Self-Counsel Press acknowledges the financial support of the Government of Canada through the Book Publishing Industry Development Program (BPIDP) for our publishing activities.

Printed in Canada.
First edition: 1987
Second edition: 1988
Third edition: 1990
Fourth edition: 1991
Fifth edition: 1993; Reprinted: 1994; 1994
Sixth edition: 1995; Reprinted: 1995; 1996
Seventh edition: 1997
Eighth edition: 1998; Reprinted: 1999 (2); 2001
Ninth edition: 2003

Canadian Cataloguing in Publication Data

Georgas, M. Stephen, 1949-
    Power of attorney kit / M. Stephen Georgas.—9th ed.

    (Self-counsel legal series)
    ISBN 1-55180-440-9

    1. Power of attorney—Canada—Popular works. 2. Power of attorney—
Canada—Forms. I. Title. II. Series.
    KE1330.G47 2003   346.7102'9   C2003-910039-1
    KF1347.Z9G47 2003

Self-Counsel Press
(a division of)
International Self-Counsel Press Ltd.

1481 Charlotte Road	1704 N. State Street
North Vancouver, BC V7J 1H1	Bellingham, WA 98225
Canada	USA

CONTENTS

SAMPLES

NOTICE TO READERS

Laws are constantly changing. Every effort is made to keep this publication as current as possible. However, neither the author nor the publisher can accept any responsibility for changes to the law or practice that occur after the printing of this publication. Please be sure that you have the most recent edition.

The donor of a power of attorney confers upon another person significant rights and powers as specified in the power of attorney and should, therefore, always obtain independent legal advice separate and apart from the attorney named in the power of attorney. In the absence of such independent legal advice, the power of attorney may be voidable.

Please note that in Samples 1 and 2, we recommend that you use a notary public or lawyer as a commissioner for taking oaths (see Chapter 2, section 3).

ACKNOWLEDGEMENTS

I would like to express my gratitude to Sandra L. Enticknap and Michelle Fernando, both of the law firm of Miller Thomson LLP, for their assistance in editing the current edition of this kit.

1
INTRODUCTION

1. WHAT IS A POWER OF ATTORNEY?

Simply stated, a power of attorney is a written document by which you grant to someone the authority to act on your behalf on various matters, including, in some provinces, matters dealing with your health. A power of attorney can be a very useful device in the management of your affairs during your lifetime, particularly as you grow older. For example, you might grant a power of attorney to your child to enable him or her to manage your affairs after a certain age.

A power of attorney is different from a will, which provides for the orderly distribution of your estate *after* your death; in most situations, a power of attorney terminates on your death.

The person who gives the authority is called the *principal* or the *donor*; the person to whom the authority is given is called the *agent, donee,* or *attorney.* You can appoint your attorney to carry out certain acts for you such as —

(a) negotiating cheques, bills of exchange, promissory notes, etc.;

(b) purchasing, selling, or dealing with stocks and bonds;

(c) collecting rents, profits, commissions, etc.;

(d) managing, buying, and selling real estate;

(e) conducting business operations; and

(f) in Ontario, Manitoba, and British Columbia, deciding issues about your personal care.

Note: The donor of a power of attorney confers on another person significant rights and powers as specified in the power of attorney and should, therefore, always obtain independent legal advice separate and apart from the attorney named in the power of attorney. In the absence of such independent legal advice, the power of attorney may be voidable.

2. AGENCY

Because the law of agency applies to powers of attorney, it is helpful to understand some of the concepts of that law.

The relationship between an agent and a principal is called an agency. An agency is created when one person, the agent, is given the authority to act on behalf of another person, the principal.

An example of an agent that many people use is a real estate agent. Generally, a real estate agent is appointed to act for a principal on certain transactions dealing with real estate. The authority is given to the real estate agent in the listing agreement and in the agreement of purchase and sale. In those documents, the agent's terms of appointment, duties, and remuneration are set out.

An agent is not an employee or an independent contractor. Legally, an employee works under the direct control and supervision of an employer and is bound to perform within the employer's guidelines and directives; an independent contractor is free to perform work as he or she sees fit and is bound only to produce the result defined by a specific contract. On the other hand, although he or she is bound to perform duties according to the principal's instructions, an agent is not normally under direct supervision like an employee, but neither is he or she free to act like an independent contractor. An agent must be instructed and guided by the agency contract.

3. HOW IS AN AGENCY CREATED?

A contract of agency or power of attorney is created when two people formalize an agreement between them. Generally, this is done by signing and sealing a document in front of a witness and having the witness swear an affidavit that he or she saw the document signed. (To "seal" a document simply means to place a small red sticker or wafer next to the signatures of the people making the contract. This practice is a holdover from the days when wax impressions were used to record a person's seal of promise. Red wafers, or seals, are available in most stationery stores.) A power of attorney is created in the document when the principal or donor gives authority to the agent or donee to act in his or her name.

4. WHO CAN BE A PRINCIPAL AND AN AGENT?

Generally, whatever you have the power to do yourself, you can do by means of an agent. Similarly, whatever you do not have the power to do yourself, cannot be done through an agent.

If you can legally enter into a contract, you may grant a power of attorney. In most cases, only the following cannot grant a power of attorney or be a principal:

(a) An enemy alien (i.e., a person whose country is at war with Canada or has hostile relations with Canada)

(b) An infant (i.e., any individual under the age of majority, subject to certain exceptions — e.g., a married person, even if an infant, can grant power of attorney. Note that the age of majority varies from province to province.)

(c) Persons of unsound mind

(d) Corporations (**Note:** A corporation's right to appoint a power of attorney can be limited by its articles of incorporation. If the articles do not permit appointment of an attorney and the appropriate legislation does not have ancillary powers to do so, the corporation cannot appoint an attorney.)

There are fewer limits on who can act as an agent or donee. Anyone other than a mental incompetent can be an agent. Therefore, an infant child could act as an agent even though he or she could not be a principal.

From a practical standpoint, I suggest that you select someone you can trust and whom you consider would be responsible in carrying out his or her duties. It is not necessary for the donee or attorney to be a lawyer.

2
LEGAL CONSIDERATIONS

1. WHAT IS IN A POWER OF ATTORNEY?

A power of attorney may be drafted to grant virtually any powers to a donee, except for certain limitations under law. For example, you could not grant to someone the power to get married on your behalf or to make your will; similarly, a judge could not delegate his or her judicial functions.

1.1 Special and general powers of attorney

A power of attorney may be either general, which extends to all kinds of business, or special, which deals with specific duties only. An example of a general power would be a document stating "to do on my behalf anything that I can lawfully do by an attorney." (See Sample 1.) Blank forms for a general power of attorney are included at the back of this booklet for your use. As well, samples of shorter forms used in some provinces are displayed in chapter 3.

An example of a special power is a document stating "to enter into an agreement of purchase and sale, and sell my property known as 123 Main Street, Anytown, British Columbia." (See Sample 2.)

Another example of a special power is when a person grants another person the power to perform banking matters. For example, elderly people, or people on vacation, may wish to appoint someone to deposit cheques or pay bills on their behalf because it is difficult or inconvenient for them to personally attend to these matters. In these cases, rather than use a general

power of attorney form, the banks usually use their own forms to be signed by the person granting the power of attorney. These forms are available at your local bank branch on request and at no charge.

Since each bank uses a slightly different form, and because the forms are available at the bank, none has been included in this kit. However, Sample 3 is an example of a banking power of attorney, and you can follow it to see how this type of form should be completed.

1.2 Administering benefits under the Old Age Security Act and Canada Pension Plan

Just as a power of attorney may be signed by elderly people for banking purposes, a similar technique is available for administering benefits under the Old Age Security Act or the Canada Pension Plan. Recipients of cheques under these plans may be too old or ill to go to the bank and cash the cheques.

In such situations, it is possible to name a trustee to receive the monthly cheques and administer the affairs of the recipient. To do so, the individual appointed to receive the monthly cheques must sign an Undertaking to Administer Benefits under the Old Age Security Act and/or the Canada Pension Plan. (See Sample 4.) As well, the individual must sign a Certificate of Incapability. (See Sample 5.) Both forms must be filed with your local office of Human Resources Development Canada — Income Security Programs. (**Note:** Even though the Undertaking to Administer

Benefits is not, technically speaking, a power of attorney, it can have the same effect.)

2. DUTIES OF THE DONEE

Whether the power is general or special, the wording in the agreement must be strictly construed and must not be interpreted in any way to extend the donee's authority beyond the agreement. If a donee does act beyond the authority given in the agreement, the act itself may be void.

In addition to the duties specified in the power of attorney, the following duties of a donee are implied unless excluded by specific wording to the contrary:

(a) The duty to use reasonable care in the performance of the acts done on behalf of the donor

(b) The duty to be accountable to the donor

(c) The duty not to make profits that the donor doesn't know about

(d) The duty not to act in conflict with the interests of the donor

3. SIGNING THE POWER OF ATTORNEY

Once both donor and donee are satisfied with the power of attorney, it must be properly signed.

When the donor signs the power of attorney, a red seal should be affixed opposite his or her name (although the seal is not absolutely necessary). Then the signature should be witnessed by two people other than the donee, the donee's spouse, the donor's spouse, or the donor's child.

The witnesses should sign the power of attorney and should swear an affidavit of subscribing witness, as shown in Samples 1 and 2. Such affidavits may be essential if the power of attorney is to be used in a land transaction under one of the provincial registry systems in your province, in which case you must meet the requirements of the relevant land registry.

Also, the notary public or lawyer before whom the witnesses swear their affidavits of subscribing witness should affix his or her notarial seal of office.

Because a donor must be the age of majority, he or she should swear an affidavit as to legal age before a lawyer or notary public. This affidavit should be attached to the power of attorney to constitute one complete document.

4. TERMINATING A POWER OF ATTORNEY

A power of attorney can be terminated in the following ways:

(a) By fulfilling a specific provision of the agreement, such as terminating on a specified date or on the occurrence of a specific event

(b) By the donor revoking the power

(c) By the donee renouncing the power

(d) By the donor going bankrupt

(e) By the death or mental incompetency of the donor (**Note:** There are some exceptions and uncertainty to this condition — see below)

4.1 Fulfilment of a specific event

The power of attorney may be terminated or expire on a certain date, if so specified, or when a particular event has occurred, such as the completion of the task for which the power of attorney was granted. In these cases, you could use clauses as follows:

This power of attorney shall be deemed to be revoked by me and terminate three months from the date hereof.

I hereby appoint Jack Green my attorney for me and on my behalf to accept an offer to purchase my house at 123 Main Street, Anytown, British

Columbia, at a price of not less than $150,000 payable in cash or by certified cheque, subject to the usual adjustments for taxes and the payment of utilities.

4.2 Revocation by the donor

A power of attorney may be revoked by the donor, unless the donor granted the power to the donee for valuable consideration (such as for the purpose of securing some benefit for the donee) and unless it is specifically stated in the power of attorney that it cannot be revoked.

The revocation need not be formal, and can even be verbal, although it is advisable that it be written. The revocation can be by the way of the donor's action, such as intervening in negotiations between the donee and a third party.

Over the course of a lifetime, you may sign several powers of attorney, so the question may arise as to which donee has power to act in a particular situation. It is generally not a donor's intention to have several powers of attorney in force, and I recommend, therefore, that any power of attorney you sign contain words of revocation such as the following:

> I hereby revoke any previous power of attorney or other delegation of authority to an agent.

Sample 6 shows a revocation of power.

4.3 Renunciation by the donee

Just as a donor may revoke a power of attorney, a donee may state that he or she does not wish to act or does not wish to act any further. This is called "renouncing the power of attorney."

A renunciation should be in writing signed by the donee, and delivered to the donor and all other persons who were dealing with the donee under the authority granted in the power of attorney. In this way, the donor and everyone else dealing with the donee will know that the donee no longer has any power and that future dealings must be conducted with the donor only.

A renunciation is shown in Sample 7.

4.4 Bankruptcy of the donor

As a general rule, a power of attorney is terminated if the donor becomes bankrupt. However, mere acts of formality by a donee in a transaction that is already binding on the donor, such as affixing seals or acknowledging receipt of money, may be performed after the donor's bankruptcy.

A donee who continues to act after notice that the donor is bankrupt risks being held personally liable, particularly if he or she sells the donor's goods and pays the proceeds to the donor.

4.5 Death or mental incompetency of donor

Subject to the principles that make a power of attorney irrevocable and the legislative provisions in some provinces, a power of attorney is terminated on the death or mental incompetency of the donor, with the following exceptions.

Under the Power of Attorney Act in Manitoba, if a power of attorney given for valuable consideration contains wording making it irrevocable, then the power is not terminated on the death of the donor.

If the donor is of unsound mind, the power of attorney is terminated, but not necessarily revoked if a third person dealing with the attorney does not know of the donor's incompetency.

However, many people have signed powers of attorney to look after their affairs only during any subsequent mental incapacity, and the legislation in British Columbia, Alberta, Saskatchewan, Manitoba, Ontario, Nova Scotia, New Brunswick, and Prince Edward Island permits a power of attorney to survive a donor's mental incapacity if there is explicit wording to that effect and if it is witnessed by someone other than the attorney or his or her spouse. There are certain restrictions in Manitoba as to who can be a witness, as well. In Ontario, as well, the power of attorney cannot be witnessed by the attorney, the spouse or partner of the donor or attorney, the donor's child, a person under the age of 18, or a person whose property is under guardianship.

The power of attorney will, however, terminate upon a committee being appointed for the donor under the Patients' Property Act of British Columbia, the Mental Health Act of Manitoba, or the Mental Health Act of Prince Edward Island.

Where a power of attorney is intended to be used *only* on the donor's subsequent mental incapacity, and no sooner, I suggest that you leave the power of attorney with your lawyer with *written* instructions that it not be released to the donee until that time. The mental incapacity of the donor could be substantiated by, for example, two written medical opinions, and only on such proof would your lawyer be obliged to turn over the power of attorney to the donee. In this manner, the chances of the power of attorney being used before it is intended are greatly reduced.

4.6 Legal advice

I am sure you can now see how a power of attorney can give a donee considerable power over your affairs, possibly not to the extent or at the time that you intended. If not properly drawn or executed, it could even be considered void and of no effect. I strongly recommend, therefore, that, prior to execution of a power of attorney, you obtain the advice of a lawyer in order to fully understand the implications of its use.

5. THE EFFECTS OF TERMINATION

5.1 General principles

If a power of attorney is terminated in any of the ways discussed above, it is important to consider the effect on the donor, donee, and any third party who relied on the power of attorney still being in force.

Once the power of attorney is terminated, the donor is no longer bound by any acts of the donee. However, to ensure this, the donor must give notice of the termination to others. Notice can be given in writing or by "constructive notice," such as by lapse of time (e.g., one or two years). If notice is not given, the donor is liable to anyone dealing with him or her through the donee on the assumption that the power of attorney still exists.

A donee who acts under a terminated power of attorney may be liable for damages to the donor, even if the donee did not know the power was no longer valid.

5.2 Provincial exceptions

In British Columbia, Alberta, Saskatchewan, and Ontario, legislation provides protection for a donee who acts in good faith without knowing that the power of attorney has been terminated. In Manitoba, the legislation states that the donee is not liable if he or she did not know or, with reasonable care, would not have known of the termination.

There are also provincial laws that define the rights and obligations of third parties who deal with a donee whose authority has been revoked. In British Columbia, if the third party and the donee have no knowledge of the power of attorney being terminated, then the donor is bound by the act of his or her donee. In Saskatchewan, the donor is bound where the third party does not know of the termination.

In Alberta, if a power of attorney is terminated or void because of the donor's mental incapacity, any exercise of the power of attorney by the donee is valid and binding in favor of a third party who did not know, or had no reasonable grounds for believing, the donee's authority had terminated.

In Manitoba, a third party is treated slightly differently. If the third party does not know of the termination, any transaction is binding provided that both the donee and the third party act in good faith.

In Prince Edward Island and in New Brunswick, a donor is bound by the actions of the donee to a third party where the donee and third party act in good faith and without knowledge that the power of attorney has been terminated.

SAMPLE 1
POWER OF ATTORNEY
(General)

POWER OF ATTORNEY

By this agreement I, _____ John Doe _____

APPOINT _____ Jack Green _____

my true and lawful attorney, for me and in my name and for my sole use and benefit to do on my behalf anything that I can otherwise lawfully do by an attorney, and without limiting the generality of the foregoing:

To purchase, rent, sell, exchange, mortgage, lease, surrender, and in every way deal with real estate, lands, and premises and any interest that I own or acquire after the effective date of this power of attorney, and execute and deliver any documents pertaining to the real estate;

To take possession of, lease, let, manage, and improve any real estate or any interest in real estate which I own or acquire after the effective date of this power of attorney, and from time to time appoint any agent to assist in managing the same, using the same power and discretion as I have if personally present;

To sell or mortgage real estate and land, and any shares, stocks, bonds, mortgages, and other securities for money, either together or in parcels, for a price by public auction, private sale, or contract as my attorney considers to be reasonable and expedient;

To execute, deliver, and acknowledge any documents and generally to deal with goods and other property and to transact all business required as my attorney sees fit, for any of the purposes mentioned here;

To deal with shares, stocks, bonds, debentures, and coupons and to vote those that have voting rights;

To negotiate with, deposit with, or transfer to any bank, any money and other negotiable notes and to endorse them on my behalf; and also to sign or endorse my name on any cheque, draft, or order for the payment of money, or to any bill of exchange or promissory note in which I have an interest; and to transact any business with the banks that may be necessary. Any bank may continue to deal with my attorney under this power until the manager or acting manager of the branch of the bank at which the account is kept receives written notice of revocation of this power of attorney. Until such notice has been given, the acts of the attorney with the bank will be binding on me;

To demand and receive from anyone all debts, in any form, which are or will be due to me;

To execute receipts and discharges of any debts owing to me when the debts have been paid;

If any person does not render a full account of the debt owing, to compel that person to do so, using all proceedings available under the law as my attorney thinks fit;

To examine and settle any account pending between me and any person;

And also for me and in my name, to enter into any agreement with any person to whom I am indebted, satisfying the debt; and generally to act as I myself could do if personally present;

To accept partial payment in satisfaction for the payment of the whole of any debt payable to me or to grant an extension of time for the payment, or otherwise to act as my attorney believes most expedient;

If any dispute arises concerning any of the matters in this power of attorney, to take the dispute to arbitration, as my attorney thinks fit, and to sign any documents for this purpose;

And also to invest or deal with any money which may be received as my attorney sees fit and in particular to buy real estate, stocks, and bonds;

And to have access to deposit and remove any documents or articles which may be in any safety deposit box I have, in any institution;

If my spouse transfers or charges any interest in a matrimonial home in which I have a right to possession under Part II of the Family Law Act of Ontario, to consent to the transaction as provided for in subparagraph 21(1)(a) of the act.

This power of attorney is subject to the following conditions and restrictions:

~~In accordance with s.2 of the Powers of Attorney Act of Alberta, I declare that the authority of my attorney under the power of attorney~~

~~(Please choose (a) or (b))~~

~~(a) is to continue notwithstanding any mental incapacity or infirmity on my part that occurs after the execution of the power of attorney.~~

~~OR~~

~~(b) is to take effect on my mental incapacity or infirmity. *~~

~~And, in accordance with s.8 of the Power of Attorney Act of British Columbia and s.10 of the Powers of Attorney Act of Manitoba and s.3 of the Power of Attorney Act of Saskatchewan, I declare that the authority of my attorney under this power of attorney will continue notwithstanding any subsequent mental infirmity on my part.~~

~~And in accordance with s.58.2 of the Property Act of New Brunswick I declare that the authority of my attorney under this power of attorney will continue notwithstanding any subsequent mental incompetence on my part. *~~

~~And, in accordance with s.3 of the Powers of Attorney Act of Nova Scotia and s.3 of the Enduring Powers of Attorney Act of Newfoundland, I declare that the authority of my attorney under this power of attorney may be exercised notwithstanding any subsequent legal incapacity on my part. *~~

*Delete any paragraphs that do not apply to you.

And, in accordance with s.7(1) of the Substitute Decisions Act of Ontario, I declare that this power of attorney may be exercised during any subsequent legal incapacity on my part. This indicates my intention that this document will be a continuing power of attorney for property under the Substitute Decisions Act, 1992, and may be used during my incapacity to manage property. I declare that, after due consideration, I am satisfied that the authority conferred on my attorney(s) named in this power of attorney is adequate to provide for the competent and effectual management of all my estate in case I should become a patient in a psychiatric facility and be certified as not competent to manage my estate under the Mental Health Act of Ontario.*

~~And, in accordance with the Powers of Attorney Act of Prince Edward Island, I declare that this power of attorney may be exercised during any subsequent legal incapacity on my part.~~*

I revoke any powers of attorney I have previously given.

I grant full power to my attorney to substitute and appoint one or more attorney(s) under him or her with the same or more limited powers, and in his or her discretion to remove this substitute.

I authorize that my attorney is to be completely indemnified against all claims, actions, and costs which may arise in connection with the exercise of this power of attorney and the administration of my estate undertaken by him or her in good faith.

In this power of attorney, where required, the singular is to be read as the plural and other grammatical changes are to be made where necessary. The word "person" includes company, corporation, body corporate, partnership, firm, or association, and the word "bank" includes trust company or person.

As witness my hand and seal at the

<u>   City   </u> of <u> Toronto   </u>)
)
this <u> 2nd </u> day of <u> January </u>, 20- <u>   </u>)   *John Doe*
)

We have signed the power of attorney in the presence of the person whose name appears above and in the presence of each other.

SIGNED, SEALED, and DELIVERED in the presence of

I. M. Witness   *J. C. Eve*
Signature   Signature

  I. M. Witness   I. C. Eve
Print name   Print name

  21 Attorney Lane   42 Attorney Lane
Address   Address

*Delete any paragraphs that do not apply to you.

AFFIDAVIT AS TO LEGAL AGE

I, _John Doe_ , of the _City of Toronto_ , in the

Province of_Ontario_ , make oath and say:

   When I signed the attached power of attorney, I was at least 18 years old.

SWORN by me at_City of Toronto_)
)
in the Province of_Ontario_ , this _2nd_ day)   _John Doe_
)   John Doe
of_January_ , 20-_____ .   )
  A. Commissioner   )
A Commissioner for taking Oaths in the Province
of_Ontario_ .

AFFIDAVIT OF WITNESS

I, _Walter Witness_ , of the _City of Toronto_ , in the

Province of_Ontario_ , make oath and say:

   I am a witness to the attached power of attorney and I was present and saw it signed at

Toronto by_John Doe_ , and I am at least 18 years of age.

   I believe that the person whose signature I witnessed is the same as that named in the power of attorney.

   I am not the attorney named in the attached power of attorney; nor am I the spouse or partner of the said attorney or the donor; nor am I the donor or child of the donor.

   I am not a person whose property is under guardianship or who has a guardian of the person.

SWORN by me at the_City of Toronto_)
)
in the Province of_Ontario_ , this_2nd_ day)   _Walter Witness_
)   Walter Witness
of_January_ , 20—_____ .   )
)
  A. Commissioner   )
A Commissioner for taking Oaths in the Province)
of_Ontario_ .   )

POWER OF ATTORNEY
(Special)

I, _____John Doe_____, of the _____City of Toronto_____,

in the Province of _____Ontario_____, appoint _____Jack Green_____,

of the _City of Vancouver_, in the Province of_____British Columbia_____,

to be my true and lawful attorney, to sell my house at_____123 Main Street_____

_____Anytown, British Columbia_____, and to discharge any related mortgages, liens, or encumbrances, and to execute all other documents and do all things which my attorney considers necessary for conveying the lands.

And I agree to confirm all my attorney does by virtue of this power of attorney.

AS WITNESS my hand and seal at the_____City of Toronto_____, in the

Province of_Ontario_____ this_2nd_ day of_January_____, 20-____.

SIGNED, SEALED, and DELIVERED	)
in the presence of	)
	) *John Doe*
	) John Doe
Walter Witness	)
Walter Witness	)
	)
Wilma Witness	)
Wilma Witness	)

AFFIDAVIT AS TO LEGAL AGE

I,_John Doe_____, of the_City of Toronto_, in the

Province of_Ontario_____, make oath and say:

When I signed the attached power of attorney, I was at least 18 years old.

SWORN by me at_City of Toronto_	)
	)
in the Province of_Ontario_, this_2nd_ day	) *John Doe*
	) John Doe
of_January_, 20-_____.	)
A. Commissioner	)
A Commissioner for taking Oaths in the Province	
of_Ontario_.	

AFFIDAVIT OF WITNESS

I, _____Walter Witness_____, of the___City of Toronto_____, in the

Province of_____Ontario_____, make oath and say:

I am a witness to the attached power of attorney and I was present and saw it signed at

_____Toronto_____ by___John Doe___, and I am at least 18 years of age.

I believe that the person whose signature I witnessed is the same as that named in the power of attorney.

I am not the attorney named in the attached power of attorney; nor am I the spouse or partner of the said attorney or the donor; nor am I the donor or child of the donor.

I am not a person whose property is under guardianship or who has a guardian of the person.

SWORN by me at the_City of Toronto___)

)

in the Province of_Ontario___, this_2nd_ day)   *Walter Witness*

)   Walter Witness

of___January___, 20—___.)

)

_A. Commissioner______)

A Commissioner for taking)

Oaths in the Province)

of_Ontario_____.)

POWER OF ATTORNEY
(Special: Banking arrangements)

This POWER OF ATTORNEY

is given on the _____ 1st _____ day of _____ February _____, 20-_____

by _____ John Doe _____

of _____ 123 Village Row, Toronto, Ontario _____

I appoint _____ M.Y. Trustworthy _____

_____ of 456 Township Street, Toronto, Ontario _____

to be my attorney to do on my behalf any of the following acts:

(a) To make, draw, accept, transfer, and endorse in favor of all parties whomsoever, all promissory notes, bills of exchange, drafts, cheques, and orders for payment of money

(b) To pay and receive all moneys and to give acquittances for the same

(c) To arrange, balance, and settle all books, accounts, and dealings

(d) To sign, give, and deliver securities under the Bank Act or otherwise and to sign, execute, issue, endorse, transfer, assign, or deliver any mortgages, hypothecation agreements, pledges, assignments, transfers, and other instruments mortgaging, hypothecating, pledging, assigning, transferring, or giving authority to sell or dispose of, or other authority over or in respect of any securities, property, goods, wares, or merchandise

(e) To borrow money from the _____ Bigge Bank of Canada _____ from time to time by way of overdraft or otherwise, with or without the pledge of security

(f) To manage and transact all manner of business whatsoever with the _____ Bigge _____

_____ Bank of Canada _____. In accordance with the Powers of Attorney Act, I declare that this power of attorney may be exercised during any subsequent legal incapacity on my part.

In accordance with the Powers of Attorney Act, I declare that, after due consideration, I am satisfied that the authority conferred on the attorney(s) named in this power of attorney is adequate to provide the competent and effectual management of all my estate in case I should become a patient in a psychiatric facility and be certified as not competent to manage my estate under the Mental Health Act.

I agree for myself, my heirs, executors, and administrators, to ratify and confirm all that my said attorney(s) shall do or cause to be done by virtue of this power of attorney. This power of attorney shall remain in full force and effect until written notice of revocation has been given to the manager or acting manager of the branch of the Biqqe Bank of Canada
in which my account is kept and receipt of such notice has been duly acknowledged in writing.

SIGNED, SEALED, and DELIVERED.

Walter Witness
Signature of witness

John Doe
Signature

Walter Witness
Name of witness

123 City Road
Toronto, Ontario
Address

Wilma Witness
Signature of witness

Wilma Witness
Name of witness

123 City Road
Toronto, Ontario
Address

SAMPLE 4
UNDERTAKING TO ADMINISTER BENEFITS UNDER THE OLD AGE SECURITY ACT AND/OR THE CANADA PENSION PLAN

Government of Canada — Income Security Programs	**Gouvernement du Canada** — Programmes de la sécurité du revenu

PROTECTED WHEN COMPLETED - A

UNDERTAKING TO ADMINISTER BENEFITS UNDER THE OLD AGE SECURITY ACT AND / OR THE CANADA PENSION PLAN ACT

The information contained on this form is essential and is used for the payment of benefits under the Old Age Security Act or Canada Pension Plan to persons on behalf of a beneficiary who is incapable of managing his/her own affairs. It is retained in the bank relating to the benefit being paid. Under the Privacy Act, the beneficiary has a right to request a copy of his record.

FOR OFFICE USE ONLY

Old Age Security Number

Social Insurance Number

OLD AGE SECURITY RECIPIENT/CANADA PENSION PLAN CONTRIBUTOR'S NAME IN FULL

Mr., Mrs., etc   Given Name and Initial   Family Name

Address (No., St., Apt. No., P O Box, R R No)   City, Town or Village

Province or Territory   Country   Postal Code

I, the undersigned, do hereby agree to receive benefits under the Old Age Security Act and / or the Canada Pension Plan Act payable to the Beneficiary or Applicant described above and undertake, pursuant to the provisions of the Old Age Security Act or the Canada Pension Plan Act, as the case may be, and the Regulations made thereunder, without charge:

1. to act on behalf of the said beneficiary and, in accordance with the directions, if any, that may be furnished to me by the Director / Regional Director of Income Security Programs, to administer and expend the benefits in the best interests of the beneficiary;

2. to account in such form and at such times as the Director / Regional Director may indicate, for all benefit payments received and the disbursements made therefrom;

3. to notify the Director / Regional Director should the beneficiary change address, become absent from Canada, die, cease to be incapable of managing his / her own affairs or should the trusteeship cease and to furnish any other information or evidence and to do anything that the Old Age Security Act and / or the Canada Pension Plan Act or the Regulations thereunder require the beneficiary to furnish or do;

4. to return uncashed, if the said beneficiary should die, all Old Age Security / or Canada Pension Plan benefit cheques in favour of the said beneficiary which remain uncashed at the time of his / her death or which may be issued subsequent to the month of death, and to indemnify Her Majesty the Queen in Right of Canada for any loss sustained by her through the cashing of such cheques.

IN WITNESS WHEREOF I execute this document under seal this _____ day of _____ 19 _____

SIGNED, SEALED AND DELIVERED in the presence of

_____
Signature of Witness

Name of Witness (Print)

Address of Witness (No., St., Apt. No., P O Box, R R No)

City, Town or Village   Province or Territory

Country   Postal Code

Occupation of Witness

_____
Signature

Name (Print)

Address (No., St., Apt. No., P O Box, R R No)

City, Town or Village   Province or Territory

Country   Postal Code

Relationship, if any, to the Beneficiary or Applicant

ISP 3506 (09-94) B   Français au verso

Canada

Government of Canada — **Gouvernement du Canada**

Income Security Programs — Programmes de la sécurité du revenu

PROTECTED WHEN COMPLETED - A

PERSONAL INFORMATION BANKS
HWC-P-PU-116
HWC-P-PU-146
HWC-P-PU-175

CERTIFICATE OF INCAPABILITY

OLD AGE SECURITY RECIPIENT/CANADA PENSION PLAN CONTRIBUTOR'S NAME IN FULL (PLEASE PRINT)

MR., MRS., ETC. USUAL FIRST OR GIVEN NAME AND INITIAL	FAMILY OR LAST NAME	SOCIAL INSURANCE NUMBER

ADDRESS (No., Street, P.O. Box, R.R. No.) — OLD AGE SECURITY NUMBER

(City, Town or Village) (Province or Territory) (Country) — AGE

PLEASE NOTE THAT IT MUST BE BY REASON OF A MENTAL ILLNESS OR A PHYSICAL ILLNESS CAUSING SEVERE MENTAL IMPAIRMENT THAT A PERSON COULD BE CONSIDERED INCAPABLE OF MANAGING HIS/HER OWN AFFAIRS

DOES APPLICANT OR BENEFICIARY HAVE:

1. RELATIVELY GOOD GENERAL KNOWLEDGE OF WHAT IS HAPPENING TO HIS/HER MONEY OR INVESTMENTS?

2. SUFFICIENT ORIENTATION TO TIME IN ORDER TO PAY BILLS?

3. SUFFICIENT MEMORY TO KEEP TRACK OF FINANCIAL TRANSACTIONS AND DECISIONS?

4. SUFFICIENT CALCULATING ABILITY TO BE ABLE TO BALANCE ACCOUNTS AND BILLS CORRECTLY?

5. SIGNIFICANT IMPAIRMENT OF JUDGEMENT DUE TO ALTERED INTELLECTUAL FUNCTION?

IN ADDITION:

6. APPROXIMATELY HOW LONG HAVE YOU KNOWN THIS PATIENT?

7. DO YOU CONSIDER THIS PERSON CAPABLE OF MANAGING HIS/HER OWN AFFAIRS? — IF NO, WHEN IS IMPROVEMENT EXPECTED?

8. DIAGNOSIS AND DATE OF ONSET

9. COMMENTS?

GIVEN NAME AND INITIAL (PRINT)	FAMILY NAME	SIGNATURE

ADDRESS (No., Street, P.O. Box, R.R. No.) — DATE

(City, Town or Village) (Province or Territory) (Country) — PROFESSION

FOR OFFICE USE ONLY

APPROVAL ☐ YES ☐ NO	REASSESSMENT DATE	SIGNATURE	DATE

ISP 3505 (09-94) B — (FRANÇAIS AU VERSO) — **Canada**

SAMPLE 6
REVOCATION OF POWER

REVOCATION OF POWER

I, John Doe , of the City of Toronto in the Province
of Ontario executed a power of attorney on the 2nd day of
January , 20- authorizing Jack Green , of the
City of Vancouver , in the Province of British Columbia , to be my
attorney, in my name, place, and stead to do all things and matters that I could lawfully do by
an attorney.

NOW, I, John Doe , for good and sufficient
reasons, do hereby revoke and cancel and make void the said power of attorney and all powers
and authority given therein, and all matters and things which shall or might be done or performed
by virtue of that power of attorney.

Dated at Vancouver this 2nd day of February , 20- .

John Doe
John Doe

SAMPLE 7
RENUNCIATION OF ATTORNEY

RENUNCIATION OF ATTORNEY

I renounce the authority granted to me by John Doe under a power of attorney
dated January 2, 20-.

Dated at Vancouver this 2nd day of February 20- .

Jack Green
Jack Green

3
PREPARING A POWER OF ATTORNEY

Besides the legal considerations discussed in chapter 2, there are also practical considerations when drafting a power of attorney. Before you consider each of the clauses below, be sure that the donor has sufficient mental capacity to sign a power of attorney and the donee understands his or her duties and obligations.

1. DRAFTING CLAUSES

In certain circumstances, you may want to consider adding clauses other than those shown in Samples 1 and 2.

1.1 Revocation

If the power of attorney does not contain a revocation clause, then any previous powers of attorney will simultaneously exist, which may authorize several donees to act. Therefore, it is wise to insert a revocation clause like the following:

> I REVOKE any powers of attorney I have previously given.

Be sure to notify the former donee of the revocation and ask that the old power of attorney be returned. It is also advisable to notify any third parties who may be relying on the previous power of attorney.

1.2 Authority to delegate acts

Except where prohibited by law, a donor may authorize the donee to delegate authority. However, a donee may not delegate authority without specific authorization, so you may want to include a clause like the following:

> I GRANT full power to my attorney to delegate any act or decision to any person as my attorney considers necessary or advisable.

1.3 Substitute attorneys

If you want to permit the donee to appoint a substitute attorney, insert a clause such as the following:

> I GRANT full power to my attorney to substitute and appoint one or more attorney(s) under him or her with the same or more limited powers, and in his or her discretion to remove this substitute.

1.4 Indemnification

An attorney (donee) is entitled to be indemnified against personal liability for acts done in good faith. Nevertheless, it may be advisable to include an indemnity in the power of attorney like the following:

> I AUTHORIZE that my attorney is to be completely indemnified against all claims, actions, and costs which may arise in connection with exercising this power of attorney and administering my estate undertaken by him or her in good faith.

1.5 Compensation

Unless it is specified in the power of attorney, an attorney probably will not be entitled to compensation for his or her acts, particularly if the donor intends the donee to act during the donor's subsequent mental incapacity. The amount of compensation may be determined by agreement or by scale for trustees or guardians set by provincial regulation.

I DECLARE that for acting as my attorney during any subsequent legal incapacity on my part, my attorney is to be entitled to compensation from my estate at the time and in the amount as my attorney and brother Robert Doe agrees, and failing agreement, as is authorized by the Trustee Act to be paid to executors and trustees acting under the last will and testament of a deceased person.

Note: In Ontario, the rules governing an attorney's compensation have changed. The attorney is entitled to compensation at a rate to be set out in law, unless the power of attorney document itself says otherwise. The amount is the same as that allowed to "guardians" of property (i.e., people who are appointed under the Substitute Decisions Act or by the Public Guardian and Trustee).

2. SPECIAL PROVINCIAL CONSIDERATIONS

The general power of attorney can be used in any province, subject to the rules of signing and witnessing documents of each province. However, when dealing with land in many provinces, other specific forms can and should be used.

2.1 British Columbia

Under the Land Title Act of British Columbia, a power of attorney cannot be registered unless the original (or, in certain cases, certified true copy) is filed and properly signed. The attorney (donee) must be at least 19 years of age, and proof of age must be given at the time of registration. (See Sample 13 for Statutory Declaration.)

A power of attorney may be revoked by filing a notice of revocation in the prescribed form (see Sample 8) or by filing such other evidence as the Registrar of Land Titles considers sufficient. A general power of attorney as shown in Sample 1 may be used or, alternatively, a short form power of attorney, shown as Form 1 in Sample 9 and Sample 11 and Form 2 in Sample 10 and Sample 12, respectively, is equally effective. Sample 9 and Sample 10 are provided in the Power of Attorney Act of British Columbia and are each equivalent to a general power of attorney. They each confer all the power on the donee that the donor could lawfully do by an attorney, subject to any limitations or restrictions which are specified in the Form 1 or Form 2, without having to set out all the powers shown in Sample 1.

Note: Sample 1, Sample 9, and Sample 10 will not be accepted in the British Columbia Land Titles office. For land-related Powers of Attorney, use Sample 11 or Sample 12. Sample 13 is to be used with Sample 11 and Sample 12 to provide proof of age. Each attorney named as the Power of Attorney in Sample 11 and Sample 12 must complete this form.

Sample 9 and Sample 11 confer authority on one attorney and Sample 10 and Sample 12 confer authority on more than one attorney acting separately or acting together, as the case may be.

A Form 1 or Form 2 may cease to be a general power of attorney if sufficient changes are made to it, so that if it has not been signed under seal and has been substantially changed so as not to resemble Form 1 and Form 2, it may have no legal effect. Therefore, if you desire to use Form 1 or Form 2, it should be prepared and signed without modifications, except for any conditions or restrictions which are permitted. Furthermore, an affidavit of age and affidavit of subscribing witness, as shown in Sample 1, should be sworn where the power of attorney is to be used outside British Columbia.

The powers of attorney shown in Sample 9, Sample 10, Sample 11, and Sample 12, as well as in Sample 1, are enduring powers of attorney in that they may be exercised during any subsequent mental incapacity of the donor.

The Representation Agreement Act, which was proclaimed into force on February 28, 2000, states that any adult can give advance directions about health care, personal care, legal matters, or financial matters by making a "Representation Agreement." This Act has brought a lot of attention to Powers of Attorney. When the Act first came in, it was intended that those aspects of the law relating to enduring Powers of Attorney would be repealed and that the representation agreement would be used to appoint someone to manage your financial, health, legal, and personal affairs. However, the government has now announced that enduring Powers of Attorney may continue to be prepared and used to manage your financial affairs.

In fact, it has now been recommended to the BC Government that the enduring Power of Attorney should be the only document that should be used for financial affairs and that Representation Agreements should be used only for your personal and health matters. At this time, however, a representation agreement can be used to appoint another person to handle both your financial and personal matters, but most people are using an enduring Power of Attorney to appoint someone for property and financial matters and a Representation Agreement to appoint someone to make decisions about health and other personal care matters.

A Representation Agreement must be in writing and be properly signed and witnessed. The person who makes decisions for you under the agreement is called a "representative." The representative must be another adult or the Public Trustee. You are allowed to designate a single representative or more than one representative. You can also appoint an alternate representative if your representative cannot act or continue to act.

If you are not capable of making a personal or health care decision yourself and if you haven't made a Representation Agreement, the Health Care (Consent) and Care Facility (Admission) Act provides that a health care provider must first contact your spouse, then children, then other relatives, in that order, to obtain necessary consents to treatment. The first qualified person contacted who agrees to make the decision (a "temporary substitute decision maker") decides on your behalf. This person may not be the person you would ordinarily choose to make health care decisions.

There are other disadvantages. There may be only one temporary substitute decision maker at any one point in time, forms must be completed, notifications must be given, and waiting periods must be adhered to. For example, when the situation involves major health care, such as major surgery or major diagnostic procedures such as an angiogram, the health care provider must first wait 72 hours after the decision has been made before providing treatment unless the treatment is required on an urgent basis. As well, a temporary substitute decision maker may make health care decisions for only 21 days from the date he or she is chosen. This means that if new types of health care are necessary beyond the 21 day period, the process of choosing a temporary substitute decision maker may have to be repeated. A temporary substitute decision maker cannot refuse life supporting care.

If you have a Representation Agreement, care can be provided without these delays and based on decisions made by a person chosen by you.

A Representation Agreement must indicate when a representative will be making health care decisions for you. It can be immediately on execution of the Representation Agreement or on a triggering event, such as a doctor's opinion that you are incapable of making your health care decisions.

The *Representation Agreement Act* includes a list of standard decision making powers with respect to health care (any of which you can include or leave out of the agreement). Standard decision making powers include decisions about —

- personal care, including where and with whom you might live, and

- major and minor health care.

There is also a list of optional decision making powers that can be included. These options may include —

- permission to restrain, move, or manage you over your objections;

- consenting to health care over your objections;

- refusing consent to specified kinds of health care, including life support; and

- accepting a proposal for your admission to a care facility.

There are two types of agreements under the Act. These are known as Section 7 agreements and Section 9 agreements. While all Representation Agreements allow you to designate the types of health care decisions that may be made on your behalf, these agreements differ in the extent of the powers granted to the representative.

If you are already having trouble managing your affairs, you need to consider a Section 7 agreement, also known as an agreement with limited powers. The level of mental capacity required to make a Section 7 agreement is lower than that required for a Section 9 agreement. You can make a Section 7 agreement containing the standard provisions noted above even though you are incapable of making a contract or managing personal, health care,

legal, business, or financial affairs. You should know, however, that a representative under a Section 7 agreement cannot refuse life supporting care. **Note:** It is not necessary to consult with a notary or lawyer to complete a Section 7, but you may want to consult with a legal professional nonetheless.

You can make a Section 9 agreement and authorize your representative to make decisions in the optional areas noted above only if you are capable of understanding the nature and effect of the authority. Under a Section 9 agreement, the representative can make any type of health care decision that may affect you, including the power to refuse life supporting care or treatment on your behalf.

When making a Representation Agreement you must decide whether or not to name someone else as a "monitor" to supervise the representative. Section 7 agreements generally require the appointment of a monitor. A monitor is not required for Section 9 agreements, although it is important to know that a Section 9 agreement must be executed after consultation with a lawyer or a notary who has taken a prescribed course of instruction.

The Act spells out the duties and powers of representatives and monitors in great detail, and representatives are required to read the provisions setting out their duties and responsibilities and to sign a certificate saying that they accept the duties and responsibilities of representative. Representatives must act in good faith and must consult with you to determine your wishes to the best extent possible. If you have made a "living will" where you have set out your wishes , your representative could consider your wishes set out in your "living will." A better alternative is to incorporate those wishes in your Representation Agreement. However, even if your wishes are not known, your representative must act in your best interest.

NOTICE OF REVOCATION OF POWER OF ATTORNEY
(British Columbia)

NOTICE OF REVOCATION OF POWER OF ATTORNEY

(British Columbia)

TO: Registrar Land Titles Office, British Columbia

The POWER OF ATTORNEY filed in your office on the __2nd__ day of __February__ , 20–__ ,

under No._____01234_____ , is revoked.

Dated the __2nd____ day of_____June_____ , 20–____ .

SIGNED IN THE PRESENCE OF:

I.M. Witness
_____
Signature

__123 Any Street, Vancouver, BC__
Address

__Business Person__
Occupation

PRINCIPAL OF POWER OF ATTORNEY

John Doe
_____
Signature

__456 A Street, Vancouver, BC__
Address

__Business Person__
Occupation

Filing Fee: Nil

Note 1: Where principal is a corporation, its seal should be affixed in presence of an authorized signatory.
Note 2: You should have someone witness your signature and swear an affidavit that he or she witnessed your signature.

Form 1
(Section 8)

POWER OF ATTORNEY

(For the appointment of one attorney)

THIS GENERAL POWER OF ATTORNEY is given on ____<u>March 2nd</u>__ 20 – ____
(Date)

by ____<u>John Doe</u>____ of ____<u>123 B Street, Vancouver</u>____
(Donor)   *(Donor's Address)*

I appoint the following person:

____<u>Jack Smith</u>____ of ____<u>321 A Street, Vancouver</u>____
(Name of Attorney)   *(Address of Attorney)*

to be my attorney in accordance with the Power of Attorney Act and to do on my behalf anything that I can lawfully do by an attorney.

(The following paragraph may be included if the donor wishes the authority granted by this power of attorney to continue despite any subsequent mental infirmity on the donor's part:)

In accordance with the Power of Attorney Act, I declare that this power of attorney may be exercised during any subsequent mental infirmity on my part.

This power of attorney is subject to the following conditions and restrictions:
(Cross this line out if there are no conditions or restrictions.)

WITNESSED BY:

<u>*I. M. Witness*</u>   )   <u>*John Doe*</u>
(Signature of Witness)   )   *(Donor)*
)
)
<u>I. M. Witness</u>   )
(Print Name of Witness)   )
)
)
<u>103 Anywhere Street, Vancouver</u>   )
(Address of Witness)   )

Note: This form is for use in British Columbia only. This form will not be accepted at the Land Titles Office.

Form 2
(Section 8)

POWER OF ATTORNEY

(For the appointment of more than one attorney)

THIS GENERAL POWER OF ATTORNEY is given on _____ March 2nd _____ 20– _____
(Date)

by _____ John Doe _____ of _____ 123 B Street, Vancouver _____
(Donor)   (Donor's Address)

I appoint the following persons:

_____ Jack Smith _____ of _____ 321 A Street, Vancouver _____
(Name of Attorney)   (Address of Attorney)

_____ Jane Black _____ of _____ 456 Any Street, Vancouver _____
(Name of Attorney)   (Address of Attorney)

(Cross out one of the following alternatives)
(who may act separately (or) who shall act together) to be my attorneys in accordance with the Power of Attorney Act and to do on my behalf anything that I can lawfully do by an attorney.

(The following paragraph may be included if the donor wishes the authority granted by this power of attorney to continue despite any subsequent mental infirmity on the donor's part:)

In accordance with the Power of Attorney Act, I declare that this power of attorney may be exercised during any subsequent mental infirmity on my part.

This power of attorney is subject to the following conditions and restrictions:
(Cross this line out if there are no conditions or restrictions.)

WITNESSED BY:

I. M. Witness)	*John Doe*
(Signature of Witness))	*(Donor)*
)	
)	
I. M. Witness)	
(Print Name of Witness))	
)	
)	
103 Anywhere Street, Vancouver)	
(Address of Witness))	

Note: This form is for use in British Columbia only. This form will not be accepted at the Land Titles Office.

POWER OF ATTORNEY — FORM 1 (LAND)
(British Columbia)

Form 1 (Land)

POWER OF ATTORNEY

(For the appointment of one attorney)

THIS GENERAL POWER OF ATTORNEY is given on the ___March 2nd___, 20–___
                                                      (Date)

by ___John Doe___ of ___123 B Street, Vancouver___.
   (Donor)   *(Donor's Address)*

I appoint the following person:

___Jack Smith___, of ___321 A Street, Vancouver___,
   (Name of Attorney)   *(Address of Attorney)*

to be my attorney in accordance with the Power of Attorney Act and to do on my behalf anything that I can lawfully do by an attorney.

(The following paragraph may be included if the donor wishes the authority granted by this power of attorney to continue despite any subsequent mental infirmity on the donor's part:)

In accordance with the Power of Attorney Act, I declare that this power of attorney may be exercised during any subsequent mental infirmity on my part.

This power of attorney is subject to the following conditions and restrictions:
(Cross this line out if there are no conditions or restrictions.)

Officer Signature(s)   *Execution Date*   *Party Signature*

Y	M	D
20–	03	02

___I. M. Notary___   ___*John Doe*___
SOLICITOR OR NOTARY PUBLIC   *(Donor)*

OFFICER CERTIFICATION:

Your signature constitutes a representation that you are a solicitor, notary public, or other person authorized by the *Evidence Act*, R.S.B.C. 1996, c. 124, to take affidavits for use in British Columbia and certifies the matters set out in Part 5 of the *Land Title Act* as they pertain to the execution of this instrument.

Note: This form is for British Columbia only.

POWER OF ATTORNEY — FORM 2 (LAND)
(British Columbia)

Form 2 (Land)

POWER OF ATTORNEY

(For the appointment of more than one attorney)

THIS GENERAL POWER OF ATTORNEY is given on the ___March 2nd___, 20-___
                                                    (Date)

by ___John Doe___, of ___123 B Street, Vancouver___.
     (Donor)   *(Donor's Address)*

I appoint the following persons:

___Jack Smith___ of ___321 A Street, Vancouver___
(Name of Attorney)   *(Address of Attorney)*

___Jane Black___ of ___456 Any Street, Vancouver___
(Name of Attorney)   *(Address of Attorney)*

(Cross out one of the following alternatives)

(who may act separately (or) who shall act together) to be my attorneys in accordance with the Power of Attorney Act and to do on my behalf anything that I can lawfully do by an attorney.

(The following paragraph may be included if the donor wishes the authority granted by this power of attorney to continue despite any subsequent mental infirmity on the donor's part.)

In accordance with the Power of Attorney Act, I declare that this power of attorney may be exercised during any subsequent mental infirmity on my part.

This power of attorney is subject to the following conditions and restrictions:
(Cross this line out if there are no conditions or restrictions.)

Officer Signature(s)	*Execution Date*			*Party Signature*
	Y	M	D	
I. M. Notary	20-	03	02	*John Doe*
SOLICITOR OR NOTARY PUBLIC				*(Donor)*

OFFICER CERTIFICATION:

Your signature constitutes a representation that you are a solicitor, notary public, or other person authorized by the *Evidence Act*, R.S.B.C. 1996, c. 124, to take affidavits for use in British Columbia and certifies the matters set out in Part 5 of the *Land Title Act* as they pertain to the execution of this instrument.

Note: This form is for use in British Columbia only.

STATUTORY DECLARATION

CANADA,

PROVINCE OF BRITISH COLUMBIA

TO WIT:

I, <u>Jack Smith</u> of <u>321 A Street, Vancouver</u>, British Columbia, <u>V0V 0V0</u> ,

DO SOLEMNLY DECLARE THAT:

1.   I am the attorney appointed by the foregoing Power of Attorney.

2.   At the time of such appointment, namely, the <u>2nd</u> day of <u>March</u> , 20-<u> </u>, I was

of the full age of nineteen years.

AND I make this solemn declaration, conscientiously believing it to be true and knowing that it is

of the same force and effect as if made under oath.

Declared before me on
<u>2nd</u> day <u>March</u> 20-<u> </u>.

	Execution Date			Party Signature
	Y	M	D	
I. M. Commissioner	20-	03	02	*Jack Smith*
Commissioner for taking oaths				

In order to make a Representation Agreement, both you and your representative must be at least 19 years of age. Each representative must sign the agreement and a certificate that he or she did not witness the agreement and that he or she accepts the duties and responsibilities of representative. If you make a Section 9 agreement and have consulted with a lawyer or a notary public who has taken the prescribed course of instruction, the lawyer or notary must sign a certificate that you appear to understand the agreement. While it has been recommended to the government that the certificates be deleted, so far they are still required. Your lawyer or notary will charge a fee for preparing your agreement, but making this type of agreement will help your representative make all the decisions you may need.

2.2 Alberta

In Alberta, the Powers of Attorney Act permits the granting of an enduring power of attorney that is, a power of attorney that may be exercised after the mental incapacity or infirmity of the donor. A power of attorney is "enduring" if the donor is an adult at the time he or she signs it and if it contains a provision that it is to continue notwithstanding any mental incapacity or infirmity of the donor after execution, or that it is to take effect only on the donor's mental incapacity or infirmity.

Under the Land Titles Act of Alberta, if a land owner wishes to have a donee take care of all the land dealings, he or she can sign a power of attorney in the prescribed form (see Sample 14). Note that the land is specifically referred to. Alternatively, a general power of attorney in which the land in question is not specifically described but is referred to in general terms may be used.

A power of attorney may be revoked by a revocation in prescribed form (see Sample 15). Where a power of attorney specifically referring to land has been filed, such as the one in Sample 14, the owner's ability to deal with the land is suspended until the revocation is filed. However, if a general power of attorney has been filed, the owner's ability to deal with the land is not suspended.

2.3 Saskatchewan

In Saskatchewan, the Land Titles Act, 2000, was recently enacted. Accompanying regulations stipulate that an authorization must accompany an application to register an assignment, amendment, or discharge of an interest. The Registrar may accept a power of attorney as authorization for registration of any application, as long as it is in a form acceptable to the Registrar. Where a power of attorney is used as authorization for an application, it must contain —

- the name of the donee;

- the name of the donor;

- a statement as to the power of the donee to deal with real property of the donor where titles or interests of the donor or instruments are referred to in general terms or any title registered in the name of the donor or any interest held by the donor or to perform any dealings on behalf of the donor; and

- the donor's signature, attested by a witness, with affidavit of execution annexed to it.

The Registrar will not accept a power of attorney as authorization for a transfer of title or assignment of interest where the transferee or assignee is the donee of the power of attorney, unless the power of attorney expressly permits the transfer or assignment to the donee.

A donor may apply to the Registrar to register an interest based on a revocation of the power of attorney. The application must specify that any power granted to the donee is revoked and state the date of the revocation, as well as include an affidavit of execution.

SAMPLE 14
POWER OF ATTORNEY FOR LAND DEALINGS
(Alberta)

FORM 20

LAND TITLES ACT
(Section 115)

POWER OF ATTORNEY

I,_____John Doe_____, being registered owner of an estate (here state nature of the estate or interest), subject to registered encumbrances, liens, and interests, if any, do hereby appoint____Jane Smith____, attorney on my behalf to (here state the nature and extent of the powers intended to be conferred, as to sell, lease, mortgage, etc.) the land described in the schedule, and to execute all instruments, and do all acts, matters, and things that may be necessary for carrying out the powers hereby given and for the recovery of all rents and sums of money that may become or are now due or owing to me in respect of the land, and for the enforcement of all contracts, covenants, or conditions binding on any lessee or occupier of the land or on any other person in respect of it, and for the taking and maintaining possession of the land, and for protecting it from waste, damage, or trespass.

In witness whereof I have hereunto subscribed my name this_____2nd_____ day of
_____May_____, 20-_____.

SIGNED by the above named__John Doe__,)

)

in the presence of   )   *John Doe*

)

   I. M. Witness   )

Note: This form is for use in Alberta only.

REVOCATION OF POWER OF ATTORNEY
(Alberta)

FORM 28
(Section 115(4))

REVOCATION OF POWER OF ATTORNEY

I,_____John Doe_____, of___Calgary_____ hereby revoke the power

of attorney given by me to___Jane Smith_____ dated the__2nd__ day of

_____May_____, 20-_____, and recorded in the Land Titles Office

at_____First Street_____for the_____Calgary_____ Land Registration

District, on the__2nd__ day of_____June_____, 20-___, as No.__007____.

In witness whereof I have hereunto subscribed my name this_____2nd_____ day of

_____June_____, 20-___.

SIGNED by the above named__John Doe___,)

)

in the presence of   )   _____*John Doe*_____

)

_____*I. M. Witness*_____)

Note: This form is for use in Alberta only.

2.4 Manitoba

The Real Property Act of Manitoba provides that a person may authorize another person to deal with his or her land, mortgage, encumbrance, or lease by power of attorney and that a registered power of attorney is not revoked by act of the parties or death of the donor until a revocation is registered. A general power of attorney may be used, and specific forms dealing with the land are not required.

2.5 Ontario

In Ontario, recent new legislation has brought a lot of attention to powers of attorney. Under the Substitute Decisions Act, which came into force April 3, 1995, you may make two types of power of attorney: a continuing power of attorney, which gives a person power to make decisions about your property and manage your finances; and a power of attorney for personal care, which allows you to appoint someone to make decisions concerning medical treatment and other personal care issues should you become mentally incapable. You may make either or both powers of attorney in Ontario. You are not necessarily required to make either of them.

Alternatively, you may also use the general power of attorney as shown in Sample

1, but you will probably find the newer, province-specific forms simpler and shorter. Rather than setting out a number of specific powers as in the general power of attorney shown in Sample 1, the continuing power of attorney for property gives broad power, subject to specific limitations which you can set out.

2.5.a Continuing power of attorney for property

Sample 16 shows a continuing power of attorney for property, which you can use to appoint a person to make decisions about your property and manage your finances. This power of attorney allows the person to continue as attorney even if you become mentally incapable. A tear-out form for a continuing power of attorney for property is also included at the back of this book.

It is important to note that not everyone can make a continuing power of attorney for property. Certain rules must be followed. The donor —

(a) must be at least 18 years old,

(b) must know what property he or she has and its approximate value,

(c) must be aware of his or her obligations to those people who depend on the donor financially,

(d) must know what his or her attorney has the authority to do,

(e) must know that his or her attorney must account for all the decisions the attorney makes about the property,

(f) must know that, if he or she is capable, the power of attorney may nevertheless be cancelled,

(g) must understand that unless the attorney manages the property prudently, its value may decline, and

(h) must understand that there is always the possibility that the attorney could misuse the authority.

There are special rules, as well, when it comes to signing the continuing power of attorney. You must sign in front of two witnesses who must be present together when you sign. Certain people are not allowed to be witnesses:

(a) The attorney or his or her spouse or partner

(b) The spouse, partner, or child of the person making the document, or someone that the person treats as his or her child

(c) A person whose property is under guardianship or who has a guardian of the person

(d) A person under the age of 18

A special feature of the Substitute Decisions Act is that it permits the grantor to make a power of attorney effective only on his or her incapacity to manage property, and not before then. Wording to the effect must be set out in the power of attorney (although the sample forms in this book do not contain such wording). If the power of attorney does not provide a method for determining when incapacity is deemed to have occurred, the power of attorney will come into effect when —

(a) the attorney is notified in prescribed form by an assessor that the assessor has performed an assessment of the grantor's capacity and has found the grantor incapable of managing property, or

(b) the attorney is notified that a certificate of incapacity has been issued for the grantor under the Mental Health Act.

Because the grantor can refuse an assessment, the power of attorney may become inoperative on his or her incapacity. Therefore, I recommend you insert a specific method for determining incapacity into the power of attorney to avoid any problems if the grantor should refuse assessment.

SAMPLE 16
CONTINUING POWER OF ATTORNEY FOR PROPERTY
(Ontario)

CONTINUING POWER OF ATTORNEY FOR PROPERTY

This general power of attorney is made in accordance with the Substitute Decisions Act, 1992.

I,_____John Doe_____, revoke any previous continuing power of attorney for property made by me.

I appoint__Jack Green_____ ~~and~~_____~~jointly/ jointly and severally,~~ to be my attorney~~(s)~~ for property.

[**Note:** *Strike out "jointly" if you want your attorneys to be able to act separately. Strike out "jointly and severally" if you want them to be legally required to make decisions together. You do not have to name more than one person.*]

I authorize my attorney~~(s)~~ for property to do on my behalf anything that I can lawfully do by an attorney and specifically anything in respect of property that I could do if capable of managing property, except make a will, subject to the law and any restrictions specified in this document.

In accordance with the Substitute Decisions Act, I declare that this power of attorney may be exercised during any subsequent legal incapacity on my part. This indicates my intention that this document will be a continuing power of attorney for property under the Substitute Decisions Act, 1992, and may be used during my incapacity to manage property.

I declare that after due consideration, I am satisfied that the authority conferred on the attorney(s) named in this power of attorney is adequate to provide for the competent and effectual management of all my estate in case I should become a patient in a psychiatric facility and be certified as not competent to manage my estate under the Mental Health Act.

Conditions and restrictions, if any:

_____

_____

_____

_____

_____

_____

_____

_____

Note: This form is for use in Ontario only.

Unless otherwise stated in this document, this continuing power of attorney will come into effect on the date it is signed and witnessed.

Unless otherwise stated in this document, I authorize my attorney(s) to take annual compensation from my property in accordance with the fee scale prescribed by regulation for the compensation of guardians of property made under section 90 of the Substitute Decisions Act, 1992.

_____*John Doe*_____   _April 3, 20-_
Signature   Date

We have signed this power of attorney in the presence of the person whose name appears above and in the presence of each other.

Witnessed by _*I. M. Witness*_   _I. M. Witness_
                  (Signature)   (Print name)

          1234 5th St., Toronto   _April 3, 20-_
                  (Address)   (Date)

Witnessed by _*I. C. Eve*_   _I. C. Eve_
                  (Signature)   (Print name)

          4232 1st St., Toronto   _April 3, 20-_
                  (Address)   (Date)

Notes: In order for this continuing power of attorney to be valid:

1. The donor must be at least 18 years old.

2. The donor must know what property he or she has and its approximate value.

3. The donor must be aware of his or her obligations to those people who depend on the donor financially.

4. The donor must know what his or her attorney has the authority to do.

5. The donor must know that his or her attorney must account for all the decisions the attorney makes about the property.

6. The donor must know that if he or she is capable, the power of attorney may nevertheless be cancelled.

POWER OF ATTORNEY FOR PERSONAL CARE
(Ontario)

POWER OF ATTORNEY FOR PERSONAL CARE

This power of attorney for personal care is made in accordance with the Substitute Decisions Act, 1992.

I, _____ John Doe _____ , revoke any previous power of attorney for personal care made by me.

I appoint _____ Jack Green _____ and _____ ~~jointly/ jointly and severally~~ to be my attorney~~(s)~~ for personal care in accordance with the Substitute Decisions Act, 1992.

[*Note: Strike out "jointly" if you want your attorneys to be able to act separately. Strike out "jointly and severally" if you want them to be legally required to make decisions together. You do not have to name more than one person.*]

I give my attorney~~(s)~~ the authority to make any personal care decisions for me that I am mentally incapable of making for myself, including the giving or refusing of consent to treatment to which the Health Care Consent Act, 1996, applies, subject to the Substitute Decisions Act, 1992, and any instructions, conditions, or restrictions contained in this form.

Instructions, conditions, and restrictions, if any :

_____

_____

_____

_____

_____

_____

_____

_____

_____*John Doe*_____   _____April 3, 20-_____
Signature   Date

Note: This form is for use in Ontario only.

We have signed this power of attorney in the presence of the person whose name appears above and in the presence of each other.

Witnessed by *I. M. Witness*
(Signature)

I. M. Witness
(Print name)

123 4th St., Toronto
(Address)

April 3, 20-
(Date)

Witnessed by *I. C. Eve*
(Signature)

I. C. Eve
(Print name)

456 7th St., Toronto
(Address)

April 3, 20-
(Date)

Notes:

1. To appoint an attorney for personal care, you must be 16 years of age or more and have the mental ability to know whether your attorney truly cares about you and that he or she may make personal care decisions for you if necessary.

2. The person you appoint must be 16 years of age or more, provided that person does not provide you with "health care or residential, social, training, advocacy, or support services for compensation," unless that person is also your spouse, partner, or relative.

3. The following people cannot be witnesses:

    (a) the attorney or his or her spouse or partner

    (b) the spouse, partner, or child of the person making the document, or someone that the person treats as his or her child

    (c) a person whose property is under guardianship or who has a guardian of the person

    (d) a person under the age of 18

Because of these new rules, I also recommend that you obtain proper legal advice if you are drafting a power of attorney in Ontario.

2.5.b Power of attorney for personal care

Sample 17 shows a power of attorney for personal care, which you can use to appoint a person to make decisions for you if you become mentally incapable. This form gives your attorney for personal care the power to decide things such as the medical treatment you receive.

If you sign a power of attorney for personal care, you must be at least 16 years of age (rather than 18 years of age) and your attorney must be at least 16 as well.

The person you appoint should be someone you trust, and must NOT be anyone who provides health care or living support services to you (unless that person is your spouse or relative). People you should NOT appoint include your doctor or landlord for example.

A tear-out form for a power of attorney for personal care in Ontario is also included at the back of this book.

2.6 New Brunswick

Under the Land Titles Act of New Brunswick, a power of attorney that describes land by its parcel index may be registered. A power of attorney that does not describe land by its parcel index may be filed with the Registrar of Land Titles but not registered.

2.7 Nova Scotia

Under the Registry Act of Nova Scotia, you must register a power of attorney with the land registry office before any document relating to a land transaction under the authority of the power of attorney can be registered.

In 1988, Nova Scotia passed the Powers of Attorney Act, which applies to powers of attorney given both before and after the act came into effect. If a power of attorney explicitly states that it may be exercised during any legal incapacity of the donor, it will not terminate upon the donor's legal incapacity, but will continue to be valid.

2.8 Prince Edward Island

The Registry Act of Prince Edward Island states that if a deed or mortgage is made and executed by virtue of a power of attorney, the power of attorney must be recorded in the registry office. Furthermore, the registration of such deed or mortgage has no force or effect until it is registered.

A general power of attorney as shown in Sample 1 may be used or a short form power of attorney or Form 1 (Sample 18), prescribed under the Powers of Attorney Act, is equally effective. Form 1 is provided in the Powers of Attorney Act of Prince Edward Island and is equivalent in effect to the general power of attorney. Form 1 confers sufficient authority on the donee to do anything that the donor can lawfully do by an attorney, subject to such limitations or restrictions as are contained in the document itself.

It is possible that Form 1 may cease to be a general power of attorney if sufficient changes are made to it, so that if it has not been signed under seal and has been significantly altered, it may have no legal effect. Therefore if Form 1 is to be used, I suggest that it not be modified in any way, except to insert any limitations or restrictions that the form itself contemplates. An affidavit of age and affidavit of subscribing witness, as shown in Sample 1, should be prepared and attached to Form 1 where the power of attorney is intended to be used outside Prince Edward Island. If the power of attorney is to be registered under the Registry Act, check with your local land titles registrar to see if any other forms or affidavits are required.

2.9 Newfoundland

The registration under the Registration of Deeds Act of an instrument executed under a power of attorney will not be valid unless the power of attorney is registered within six months after registration of the document or unless a document subsequently confirming the execution of the first instrument is registered within the same six-month period.

Newfoundland passed the Enduring Powers of Attorney Act in June 1990. As in many of the other provinces, the power of attorney will survive any subsequent legal incapacity of the donor if the power of attorney contains a provision to that effect.

A person must be 19 years of age or older to be named as an attorney.

Where a power of attorney is terminated or revoked, and the attorney continues to act in good faith without knowledge of the termination or revocation and in accordance with the provisions of the power of attorney, the attorney will be considered to have had authority to act. Furthermore, any dealing with a third party who did not know of the termination or revocation will be considered valid.

2.10 Yukon

The Yukon territory enacted the Enduring Power of Attorney Act in 1995, which is unique compared to corresponding legislation enacted by the provinces. The Yukon Act states that a power of attorney is an enduring power of attorney if —

- the donor is an adult at the time of execution;

- the power of attorney is in writing, dated, and signed by the donor;

- the power contains a statement that the power continues notwithstanding any mental incapacity of the donor or is to take effect on the mental incapacity of the donor;

- the power incorporates the explanatory notes set out in the Schedule; and

- the power is accompanied by certificates of legal advice provided to the donee and to the donor.

2.11 Northwest Territories

With the enactment of the Powers of Attorney Act in 2001, the Land Titles Act underwent amendment. It now states that where a person authorizes and appoints any person to act for or on behalf of the person with respect to the transfer or other dealing with land through a power of attorney, the power of attorney may be filed in a land titles office. Where a Registrar is satisfied that there is sufficient evidence to conclude that the power of attorney has been revoked or terminated, the Registrar may file the revocation or a notice of the termination in the general register.

3. SUMMARY

It may happen that a power of attorney signed in one province will be used in another province where the land to be dealt with is located. Because the forms may vary from province to province, I suggest that you use a general power of attorney in which the land in question is referred to, but not specifically described, together with an Affidavit as to Legal Age of the donor and an Affidavit of Subscribing Witness. Both affidavits should be sworn before a notary public in the province in which the power of attorney is executed, with his or her notarial seal affixed.

By following this procedure, your power of attorney should be valid in all Canadian provinces. However, when in doubt, I suggest you consult your lawyer or nearest government land registry office for assistance.

The forms used in specific cases by province, referred to above, may be available in your local stationery store, or you may typewrite them yourself. Contact your local government land registry office for further information.

SAMPLE 18
FORM OF POWER OF ATTORNEY
(Prince Edward Island)

FORM 1

FORM OF POWER OF ATTORNEY

THIS GENERAL POWER OF ATTORNEY is given on ___January 2nd___ 20-___
                                                        (Date)

by ___John Doe___ of ___123 B Street, Charlottetown___
        (Donor)   *(Donor's Address)*

I appoint ___Jack Green___ of ___456 C Street, Charlottetown___
              (Attorney)   *(Address of Attorney)*

~~(or~~ _____ ~~of~~ _____
              (Attorney)   *(Address of Attorney)*

~~and~~ _____ ~~of~~ _____)
              (Attorney)   *(Address of Attorney)*

~~jointly (or jointly and severally)~~ to be my attorney(s) in accordance with the Power of Attorney Act and to do on my behalf anything that I can lawfully do by an attorney.

(The following paragraph may be included if the donor wishes the authority granted by this power of attorney to continue notwithstanding any subsequent mental infirmity on his or her part:)

In accordance with the Power of Attorney Act, I declare that this power of attorney may be exercised during any subsequent legal incapacity on my part.

This power of attorney is subject to the following conditions and restrictions:

WITNESSED BY:

_____*I. M. Witness*_____)
(Signature of Witness))
)
)
___I. M. Witness___   )   ___*John Doe*___
(Print Name of Witness))   *(Donor)*
)
___1000 Blue St., Charlottetown___)
(Address of Witness)   )

Note: This form is for use in Prince Edward Island only.

POWER OF ATTORNEY

By this agreement I, _____

APPOINT _____

my true and lawful attorney, for me and in my name and for my sole use and benefit to do on my behalf anything that I can otherwise lawfully do by an attorney, and without limiting the generality of the foregoing:

To purchase, rent, sell, exchange, mortgage, lease, surrender, and in every way deal with real estate, lands, and premises and any interest that I own or acquire after the effective date of this power of attorney, and execute and deliver any documents pertaining to the real estate;

To take possession of, lease, let, manage, and improve any real estate or any interest in real estate which I own or acquire after the effective date of this power of attorney, and from time to time appoint any agent to assist in managing the same, using the same power and discretion as I have if personally present;

To sell or mortgage real estate and land, and any shares, stocks, bonds, mortgages, and other securities for money, either together or in parcels, for a price by public auction, private sale, or contract as my attorney considers to be reasonable and expedient;

To execute, deliver, and acknowledge any documents and generally to deal with goods and other property and to transact all business required as my attorney sees fit, for any of the purposes mentioned here;

To deal with shares, stocks, bonds, debentures, and coupons and to vote those that have voting rights;

To negotiate with, deposit with, or transfer to any bank, any money and other negotiable notes and to endorse them on my behalf; and also to sign or endorse my name on any cheque, draft, or order for the payment of money, or to any bill of exchange or promissory note in which I have an interest; and to transact any business with the banks that may be necessary. Any bank may continue to deal with my attorney under this power until the manager or acting manager of the branch of the bank at which the account is kept receives written notice of revocation of this power of attorney. Until such notice has been given, the acts of the attorney with the bank will be binding on me;

To demand and receive from anyone all debts, in any form, which are or will be due to me;

To execute receipts and discharges of any debts owing to me when the debts have been paid;

If any person does not render a full account of the debt owing, to compel that person to do so, using all proceedings available under the law as my attorney thinks fit;

To examine and settle any account pending between me and any person;

And also for me and in my name, to enter into any agreement with any person to whom I am indebted, satisfying the debt; and generally to act as I myself could do if personally present;

To accept partial payment in satisfaction for the payment of the whole of any debt payable to me or to grant an extension of time for the payment, or otherwise to act as my attorney believes most expedient;

If any dispute arises concerning any of the matters in this power of attorney, to take the dispute to arbitration, as my attorney thinks fit, and to sign any documents for this purpose;

And also to invest or deal with any money which may be received as my attorney sees fit and in particular to buy real estate, stocks, and bonds;

And to have access to deposit and remove any documents or articles which may be in any safety deposit box I have, in any institution;

If my spouse transfers or charges any interest in a matrimonial home in which I have a right to possession under Part II of the Family Law Act of Ontario, to consent to the transaction as provided for in subparagraph 21(1)(a) of the act.

This power of attorney is subject to the following conditions and restrictions:

[*insert conditions and restrictions here*]

In accordance with s.2 of the Powers of Attorney Act of Alberta, I declare that the authority of my attorney under the power of attorney —

(a)   is to continue notwithstanding any mental incapacity or infirmity on my part that occurs after the execution of the power of attorney.

OR

(b)   is to take effect on my mental incapacity or infirmity. *

Please
choose
(a) or (b)

And, in accordance with s.8 of the Power of Attorney Act of British Columbia and s.10 of the Powers of Attorney Act of Manitoba and s.3 of the Power of Attorney Act of Saskatchewan, I declare that the authority of my attorney under this power of attorney will continue notwithstanding any subsequent mental infirmity on my part. *

And, in accordance with s.58.2 of the Property Act of New Brunswick, I declare that the authority of my attorney under this power of attorney will continue notwithstanding any subsequent mental incompetence on my part.*

And, in accordance with s.3 of the Powers of Attorney Act of Nova Scotia and s.3 of the Enduring Powers of Attorney Act of Newfoundland, I declare that the authority of my attorney under this power of attorney may be exercised notwithstanding any subsequent legal incapacity on my part. *

And, in accordance with s.7(1) of the Substitute Decisions Act of Ontario, I declare that this power of attorney may be exercised during any subsequent legal incapacity on my part. This indicates my intention that this document will be a continuing power of attorney for property under the Substitute Decisions Act, 1992, and may be used during my incapacity to manage property. I declare that, after due consideration, I am satisfied that the authority conferred on my attorney(s) named in this power of attorney is adequate to provide for the competent and effectual management of all my estate in case I should become a patient in a psychiatric facility and be certified as not competent to manage my estate under the Mental Health Act of Ontario. *

And, in accordance with the Powers of Attorney Act of Prince Edward Island, I declare that this power of attorney may be exercised during any subsequent legal incapacity on my part. *

I revoke any powers of attorney I have previously given.

I grant full power to my attorney to substitute and appoint one or more attorney(s) under him or her with the same or more limited powers, and in his or her discretion to remove this substitute.

I authorize that my attorney is to be completely indemnified against all claims, actions, and costs which may arise in connection with the exercise of this power of attorney and the administration of my estate undertaken by him or her in good faith.

---

* Delete any paragraphs that do not apply to you.

In this power of attorney, where required, the singular is to be read as the plural and other grammatical changes are to be made where necessary. The word "person" includes company, corporation, body corporate, partnership, firm, or association, and the word "bank" includes trust company or person.

As witness my hand and seal at the

_____ of_____)

)

this_____ day of_____, 20_____)

)

_____)

)

_____

We have signed the power of attorney in the presence of the person whose name appears above and in the presence of each other.

SIGNED, SEALED, and DELIVERED in the presence of

_____   _____
Signature   Signature

_____   _____
Print name   Print name

_____   _____
Address   Address

AFFIDAVIT AS TO LEGAL AGE

I,_____, of the_____, in the

Province of_____, make oath and say:

When I signed the attached power of attorney, I was at least 18 years old.

SWORN by me at_____)
)

in the Province of_____, this_____ day)   _____
)

of_____, 20_____.   )
)

_____)

AFFIDAVIT OF WITNESS

I,_____, of the_____, in the

Province of_____, make oath and say:

I am a witness to the attached power of attorney and I was present and saw it signed at

_____ by_____, and I am at least 18 years of age.

I believe that the person whose signature I witnessed is the same as that named in the power of attorney.

I am not the attorney named in the attached power of attorney; nor am I the spouse or partner of the said attorney or the donor; nor am I the donor or child of the donor.

I am not a person whose property is under guardianship or who has a guardian of the person.

SWORN by me at_____)
)
in the Province of_____, this_____ day)   _____
)
of_____, 20_____.   )
)
_____   )
A Commissioner for taking
Oaths in the Province
of_____.   )

CONTINUING POWER OF ATTORNEY FOR PROPERTY

This general power of attorney is made in accordance with the Substitute Decisions Act, 1992.

I,_____, revoke any previous continuing power of attorney for property made by me.

I appoint_____ and_____ jointly/ jointly and severally, to be my attorney(s) for property.

[**Note:** *Strike out "jointly" if you want your attorneys to be able to act separately. Strike out "jointly and severally" if you want them to be legally required to make decisions together. You do not have to name more than one person.*]

I authorize my attorney(s) for property to do on my behalf anything that I can lawfully do by an attorney and specifically anything in respect of property that I could do if capable of managing property, except make a will, subject to the law and any restrictions specified in this document.

In accordance with the Substitute Decisions Act, I declare that this power of attorney may be exercised during any subsequent legal incapacity on my part. This indicates my intention that this document will be a continuing power of attorney for property under the Substitute Decisions Act, 1992, and may be used during my incapacity to manage property.

I declare that after due consideration, I am satisfied that the authority conferred on the attorney(s) named in this power of attorney is adequate to provide for the competent and effectual management of all my estate in case I should become a patient in a psychiatric facility and be certified as not competent to manage my estate under the Mental Health Act.

Conditions and restrictions, if any:

_____

_____

_____

_____

_____

_____

_____

_____

Note: This form is for use in Ontario only.

SELF-COUNSEL PRESS-CDN-PAT-ON(4-1)03

Unless otherwise stated in this document, this continuing power of attorney will come into effect on the date it is signed and witnessed.

Unless otherwise stated in this document, I authorize my attorney(s) to take annual compensation from my property in accordance with the fee scale prescribed by regulation for the compensation of guardians of property made under section 90 of the Substitute Decisions Act, 1992.

_____   _____

Signature   Date

We have signed this power of attorney in the presence of the person whose name appears above and in the presence of each other.

Witnessed by _____   _____
                    (Signature)   (Print name)

             _____   _____
                    (Address)   (Date)

Witnessed by _____   _____
                    (Signature)   (Print name)

             _____   _____
                    (Address)   (Date)

Notes: In order for this continuing power of attorney to be valid:

1. The donor must be at least 18 years old.

2. The donor must know what property he or she has and its approximate value.

3. The donor must be aware of his or her obligations to those people who depend on the donor financially.

4. The donor must know what his or her attorney has the authority to do.

5. The donor must know that his or her attorney must account for all the decisions the attorney makes about the property.

6. The donor must know that if he or she is capable, the power of attorney may nevertheless be cancelled.

POWER OF ATTORNEY FOR PERSONAL CARE

This power of attorney for personal care is made in accordance with the Substitute Decisions Act, 1992.

I,_____ , revoke any previous power of attorney for personal care made by me.

I appoint_____ and_____ jointly/ jointly and severally to be my attorney(s) for personal care in accordance with the Substitute Decisions Act, 1992.

[**Note:** *Strike out "jointly" if you want your attorneys to be able to act separately. Strike out "jointly and severally" if you want them to be legally required to make decisions together. You do not have to name more than one person.*]

I give my attorney(s) the authority to make any personal care decisions for me that I am mentally incapable of making for myself, including the giving or refusing of consent to treatment to which the Health Care Consent Act, 1996, applies, subject to the Substitute Decisions Act, 1992, and any instructions, conditions, or restrictions contained in this form.

Instructions, conditions, and restrictions, if any :

_____

_____

_____

_____

_____

_____

_____

_____

_____   _____
Signature   Date

Note: This form is for use in Ontario only.

We have signed this power of attorney in the presence of the person whose name appears above and in the presence of each other.

Witnessed by _____   _____
                      (Signature)   (Print name)

                       _____   _____
                      (Address)   (Date)

Witnessed by _____   _____
                      (Signature)   (Print name)

                       _____   _____
                      (Address)   (Date)

Notes:

1. To appoint an attorney for personal care, you must be 16 years of age or more and have the mental ability to know whether your attorney truly cares about you and that he or she may make personal care decisions for you if necessary.

2. The person you appoint must be 16 years of age or more, provided that person does not provide you with "health care or residential, social, training, advocacy, or support services for compensation," unless that person is also your spouse, partner, or relative.

3. The following people cannot be witnesses:

    (a) the attorney or his or her spouse or partner

    (b) the spouse, partner, or child of the person making the document, or someone that the person treats as his or her child

    (c) a person whose property is under guardianship or who has a guardian of the person

    (d) a person under the age of 18

POWER OF ATTORNEY
(Special)

I,_____, of the_____,

in the Province of_____, appoint_____,

of the_____, in the Province of_____,

to be my true and lawful attorney, to sell my house at_____

_____, and to discharge any related
mortgages, liens, or encumbrances, and to execute all other documents and do all things which
my attorney considers necessary for conveying the lands.

    And I agree to confirm all my attorney does by virtue of this power of attorney.

    AS WITNESS my hand and seal at the_____, in the

Province of_____ this_____ day of_____, 20_____.

SIGNED, SEALED, and DELIVERED   )
in the presence of   )
)   _____
)
_____)
Name of Witness   )
)
_____)
Name of Witness   )

POWER OF ATTORNEY
(Special: Banking arrangements)

This POWER OF ATTORNEY

is given on the_____ day of_____, 20_____

by_____

of_____

I appoint_____

_____

to be my attorney to do on my behalf any of the following acts:

   (a)   To make, draw, accept, transfer, and endorse in favor of all parties whomsoever, all promissory notes, bills of exchange, drafts, cheques, and orders for payment of money

   (b)   To pay and receive all moneys and to give acquittances for the same

   (c)   To arrange, balance, and settle all books, accounts, and dealings

   (d)   To sign, give, and deliver securities under the Bank Act or otherwise and to sign, execute, issue, endorse, transfer, assign, or deliver any mortgages, hypothecation agreements, pledges, assignments, transfers, and other instruments mortgaging, hypothecating, pledging, assigning, transferring, or giving authority to sell or dispose of, or other authority over or in respect of any securities, property, goods, wares, or merchandise

   (e)   To borrow money from the_____ from time to time by way of overdraft or otherwise, with or without the pledge of security

   (f)   To manage and transact all manner of business whatsoever with the_____

_____. In accordance with the Powers of Attorney Act, I declare that this power of attorney may be exercised during any subsequent legal incapacity on my part.

In accordance with the Powers of Attorney Act, I declare that, after due consideration, I am satisfied that the authority conferred on the attorney(s) named in this power of attorney is adequate to provide the competent and effectual management of all my estate in case I should become a patient in a psychiatric facility and be certified as not competent to manage my estate under the Mental Health Act.

I agree for myself, my heirs, executors, and administrators, to ratify and confirm all that my said attorney(s) shall do or cause to be done by virtue of this power of attorney. This power of attorney shall remain in full force and effect until written notice of revocation has been given to the manager or acting manager of the branch of the_____

in which my account is kept and receipt of such notice has been duly acknowledged in writing.

SIGNED, SEALED, and DELIVERED.

_____
Signature of witness

_____
Signature

_____
Name of witness

_____
Address

_____
Signature of witness

_____
Name of witness

_____
Address

REVOCATION OF POWER

I,_____, of the_____in the Province

of_____ executed a power of attorney on the_____ day of

_____, 20_____ authorizing_____, of the

_____, in the Province of_____, to be my

attorney, in my name, place, and stead to do all things and matters that I could lawfully do by
an attorney.

NOW, I,_____, for good and sufficient
reasons, do hereby revoke and cancel and make void the said power of attorney and all powers
and authority given therein, and all matters and things which shall or might be done or performed
by virtue of that power of attorney.

Dated at_____ this_____ day of_____, 20_____.

_____

RENUNCIATION OF ATTORNEY

I renounce the authority granted to me by_____

under a power of attorney dated_____.

    Dated at_____ this_____ day of_____ 20_____.

_____

NOTICE OF REVOCATION OF POWER OF ATTORNEY

TO: Registrar Land Titles Office, British Columbia

The POWER OF ATTORNEY filed in your office on the_____ day of_____, 20____,

under No._____, is revoked.

Dated the_____ day of_____, 20_____.

SIGNED IN THE PRESENCE OF:

_____
Signature

_____
Address

_____
Occupation

PRINCIPAL OF POWER OF ATTORNEY

_____
Signature

_____
Address

_____
Occupation

Filing Fee: Nil

Form 1
(Section 8)

POWER OF ATTORNEY
(For the appointment of one attorney)

THIS GENERAL POWER OF ATTORNEY is given on_____20_____

(Date)

by_____of_____

(Donor)   *(Donor's Address)*

I appoint the following person:

_____of_____

(Name of Attorney)   *(Address of Attorney)*

to be my attorney in accordance with the Power of Attorney Act and to do on my behalf anything that I can lawfully do by an attorney.

(The following paragraph may be included if the donor wishes the authority granted by this power of attorney to continue despite any subsequent mental infirmity on the donor's part:)

In accordance with the Power of Attorney Act, I declare that this power of attorney may be exercised during any subsequent mental infirmity on my part.

This power of attorney is subject to the following conditions and restrictions:
(Cross this line out if there are no conditions or restrictions.)

WITNESSED BY:

_____)

(Signature of Witness)   )   _____

)   *(Donor)*

)

)

)

_____)

(Print Name of Witness)   )

)

)

_____)

(Address of Witness)   )

Note: This form is for use in British Columbia only. This form will not be accepted at the Land Titles Office.

Form 2

(Section 8)

POWER OF ATTORNEY

(For the appointment of more than one attorney)

THIS GENERAL POWER OF ATTORNEY is given on_____20____

(Date)

by_____of_____

(Donor)   (Donor's Address)

I appoint the following persons:

_____ of_____

(Name of Attorney)   (Address of Attorney)

_____ of_____

(Name of Attorney)   (Address of Attorney)

(Cross out one of the following alternatives)

(who may act separately (or) who shall act together) to be my attorneys in accordance with the Power of Attorney Act and to do on my behalf anything that I can lawfully do by an attorney.

(The following paragraph may be included if the donor wishes the authority granted by this power of attorney to continue despite any subsequent mental infirmity on the donor's part:)

In accordance with the Power of Attorney Act, I declare that this power of attorney may be exercised during any subsequent mental infirmity on my part.

This power of attorney is subject to the following conditions and restrictions:
(Cross this line out if there are no conditions or restrictions.)

WITNESSED BY:

_____) _____

(Signature of Witness)   )   (Donor)

)
)
)

_____)

(Print Name of Witness)   )

)
)

_____)

(Address of Witness)   )

Note: This form is for use in British Columbia only. This form will not be accepted at the Land Titles Office.

Form 1 (Land)

POWER OF ATTORNEY
(For the appointment of one attorney)

THIS GENERAL POWER OF ATTORNEY is given on the _____, 20_____
(Date)

by _____ of _____.
(Donor)   (Donor's Address)

I appoint the following person:

_____, of _____,
(Name of Attorney)   (Address of Attorney)

to be my attorney in accordance with the Power of Attorney Act and to do on my behalf anything that I can lawfully do by an attorney.

(The following paragraph may be included if the donor wishes the authority granted by this power of attorney to continue despite any subsequent mental infirmity on the donor's part:)

In accordance with the Power of Attorney Act, I declare that this power of attorney may be exercised during any subsequent mental infirmity on my part.

This power of attorney is subject to the following conditions and restrictions: *(Cross this line out if there are no conditions or restrictions.)*

Officer Signature(s)	*Execution Date*			*Party Signature*
	Y	M	D	
_____	—	—	—	_____
SOLICITOR OR NOTARY PUBLIC				*(Donor)*

OFFICER CERTIFICATION:

Your signature constitutes a representation that you are a solicitor, notary public, or other person authorized by the *Evidence Act*, R.S.B.C. 1996, c. 124, to take affidavits for use in British Columbia and certifies the matters set out in Part 5 of the *Land Title Act* as they pertain to the execution of this instrument.

Note: This form is for British Columbia only.

STATUTORY DECLARATION

CANADA,

PROVINCE OF BRITISH COLUMBIA

TO WIT:

I,_____of _____, British Columbia, _____,

DO SOLEMNLY DECLARE THAT:

1.   I am the attorney appointed by the foregoing Power of Attorney.

2.   At the time of such appointment, namely, the____ day of _____, 20____, I was

of the full age of nineteen years.

AND I make this solemn declaration, conscientiously believing it to be true and knowing that it is
of the same force and effect as if made under oath.

Declared before me on

_____ day_____ 20_____.

Execution Date			*Party Signature*
Y	M	D	
—	—	—	

_____

Commissioner for taking oaths

Form 2 (Land)

POWER OF ATTORNEY
(For the appointment of more than one attorney)

THIS GENERAL POWER OF ATTORNEY is given on the _____, 20_____
                                                              (Date)

by _____, of _____.
          (Donor)   *(Donor's Address)*

I appoint the following persons:

_____ of _____
          (Name of Attorney)   *(Address of Attorney)*

_____ of _____
          (Name of Attorney)   *(Address of Attorney)*

(Cross out one of the following alternatives)

(who may act separately (or) who shall act together) to be my attorneys in accordance with the Power of Attorney Act and to do on my behalf anything that I can lawfully do by an attorney.

(The following paragraph may be included if the donor wishes the authority granted by this power of attorney to continue despite any subsequent mental infirmity on the donor's part.)

In accordance with the Power of Attorney Act, I declare that this power of attorney may be exercised during any subsequent mental infirmity on my part.

This power of attorney is subject to the following conditions and restrictions:
(Cross this line out if there are no conditions or restrictions.)

Officer Signature(s)	Execution Date			*Party Signature*
	Y	M	D	

_____   —   —   —   _____
SOLICITOR OR NOTARY PUBLIC   *(Donor)*

OFFICER CERTIFICATION:

Your signature constitutes a representation that you are a solicitor, notary public, or other person authorized by the *Evidence Act*, R.S.B.C. 1996, c. 124, to take affidavits for use in British Columbia and certifies the matters set out in Part 5 of the *Land Title Act* as they pertain to the execution of this instrument.

Note: This form is for use in British Columbia only.

STATUTORY DECLARATION

CANADA,

PROVINCE OF BRITISH COLUMBIA

TO WIT:

I,_____of _____, British Columbia, _____,

DO SOLEMNLY DECLARE THAT:

1.   I am the attorney appointed by the foregoing Power of Attorney.

2.   At the time of such appointment, namely, the_____ day of _____, 20_____,

I was of the full age of nineteen years.

AND I make this solemn declaration, conscientiously believing it to be true and knowing that it is

of the same force and effect as if made under oath.

Declared before me on
_____ day_____ 20_____.

Execution Date

Y	M	D
—	—	—

Party Signature

_____
Commissioner for taking oaths

_____

FORM 20

LAND TITLES ACT
(Section 115)

POWER OF ATTORNEY

I,_____, being registered owner of an estate (here state

nature of the estate or interest), subject to registered encumbrances, liens, and interests, if any,
do hereby appoint_____, attorney on my behalf to (here state the nature
and extent of the powers intended to be conferred, as to sell, lease, mortgage, etc.) the land
described in the schedule, and to execute all instruments, and do all acts, matters, and things
that may be necessary for carrying out the powers hereby given and for the recovery of all
rents and sums of money that may become or are now due or owing to me in respect of the
land, and for the enforcement of all contracts, covenants, or conditions binding on any lessee
or occupier of the land or on any other person in respect of it, and for the taking and
maintaining possession of the land, and for protecting it from waste, damage, or trespass.

In witness whereof I have hereunto subscribed my name this_____ day of

_____, 20____.

SIGNED by the above named_____,)
)

 in the presence of   )   _____

)

_____)

Note: This form is for use in Alberta only.

FORM 28
(Section 115(4))

REVOCATION OF POWER OF ATTORNEY

I,_____, of_____ hereby revoke the power

of attorney given by me to_____ dated the_____ day of

_____, 20_____, and recorded in the Land Titles Office

at_____for the_____ Land Registration

District, on the_____ day of_____, 20____, as No._____.

In witness whereof I have hereunto subscribed my name this_____ day of

_____, 20____.

SIGNED by the above named_____,)
)
 in the presence of   )   _____
)
_____)

Note: This form is for use in Alberta only.

FORM 1

FORM OF POWER OF ATTORNEY

THIS GENERAL POWER OF ATTORNEY is given on_____
(Date)

by_____ of_____
(Donor) *(Donor's Address)*

I appoint_____ of_____
(Attorney) *(Address of Attorney)*

(or_____ of_____
(Attorney) *(Address of Attorney)*

and_____ of_____)
(Attorney) *(Address of Attorney)*

jointly (or jointly and severally) to be my attorney(s) in accordance with the Power of Attorney Act and to do on my behalf anything that I can lawfully do by an attorney.

(The following paragraph may be included if the donor wishes the authority granted by this power of attorney to continue notwithstanding any subsequent mental infirmity on his or her part:)

> In accordance with the Power of Attorney Act, I declare that this power of attorney may be exercised during any subsequent legal incapacity on my part.

This power of attorney is subject to the following conditions and restrictions:

WITNESSED BY:

_____)
(Signature of Witness))
)
)
_____)
(Print Name of Witness))   _____
)   *(Donor)*
_____)
(Address of Witness))

Note: This form is for use in Prince Edward Island only.